IN SEARCH OF THE UNEXPLAINED

GHOSTS

by Jenna Lee Gleisner

The Quest for Discovery Never Ends

This edition first published in 2022 by Kaleidoscope Publishing, Inc.

No part of this publication may be reproduced in whole or in part without written permission of the publisher.

For information regarding permission, write to Kaleidoscope Publishing, Inc.
6012 Blue Circle Drive
Minnetonka, MN 55343

Library of Congress Control Number
2021934875

ISBN
978-1-64519-485-9 (library bound)
978-1-64519-523-8 (ebook)

FIND ME IF YOU CAN!

Bigfoot lurks within one of the images in this book. It's up to you to find him!

TABLE OF
CONTENTS

FLICKERING LIGHTS

"**J**ust one more paragraph and we're done, guys," says Becca. They've been working all day on this group project.

"Mr. Smith was nice enough to let us stay late, but I'm ready to be done," replies Jonah.

"I'm just glad we'll get it turned in on time," says Steph. Just then, the library lights start to **flicker**.

"Hello?" ask the students. "We're still in here!" But the lights keep flickering. Some go completely dark. Then the door to the hallway slams shut.

"Are any of the other groups still working?" asks Jonah.

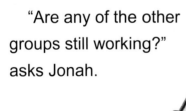

"They must be playing a trick on us." But then a book on the table next to them falls to the floor.

"Let's get out of here!" The students bolt out of the library and out of the school. All three saw the lights flicker and heard the door shut. And there's no mistaking that the book fell to the floor. Did it fall by itself? Or was the school ghost telling them to go home?

Chapter 1

LIVING SOULS

Dating back to ancient times, people have believed that the souls of the dead can remain on Earth. Ghosts are souls or spirits that can appear, and sometimes **interact** with, the living. Some people claim to see these spirits as shapes or shadowy figures. Others claim they hear their voices, screams, or laughter. And others, like the kids in the school library, claim they experience **paranormal** activity. Doors slam shut and lights flicker, turn on, or turn off—all on their own. Others don't see ghosts, but they **sense** them.

FUN FACT

One in five Americans say they've seen a ghost or experienced paranormal activity.

There is no scientific **evidence** that ghosts are real. But how can we explain paranormal activity? Believers say spirits need energy to **manifest**. They may take it from an electrical source, such as lights. This power draw could explain flickering lights. What do you think? After we die, could our souls manifest into ghosts? Are ghosts real? Decide for yourself as we go in search of the unexplained!

EXPERT EXPLANATION

It can be easy to blame ghosts for flickering lights or moving objects when we can't see anyone behind the actions. But experts have a different opinion. Even though we can't see the cause, they believe there is a reason behind the actions. Flickering lights could mean electrical problems or bad wiring. Slamming doors or falling objects could simply be the wind at play.

Chapter 2

FLOATING FIGURES

"**L**et's take another one," says Liza. Her friend, Maya, moves her phone and takes another photo.

"OK, I just sent it to you," says Maya. "See you tomorrow!" The girls part ways after school.

After dinner, Liza checks her phone and opens the photo. She gasps when she sees it: Right behind her in the picture is what looks like another kid. They were alone outside the school earlier. She calls Maya.

"Did you photoshop someone else into that photo?" asks Liza.

"No, why would I do that?" Maya answers.

"Look at the picture again," Liza says.

After moments of silence, Maya replies in almost a whisper, "Who is that?"

What Liza and Maya saw in their photo is known as an **apparition**. Sometimes an apparition can look just like a real person. They are often clothed. They look so real people can describe their hair and facial features. Oftentimes, they are **translucent**. They are described as cloudy and white, gray, or even black. Sometimes, these figures show up in photos.

FUZZY PHOTOS

While many claim to have photo or video evidence of ghosts, experts say there are scientific explanations. Moving apparitions in videos could be cobwebs or insects flying in front of camera lenses. Spots or figures in photos could be dust particles. Since phones often take photos in stages, anything moving through the shot could appear distorted.

People claim to see ghosts of all ages doing all sorts of things. Ghosts of children are seen running and playing in schoolyards. Elderly ghosts are seen walking cemeteries at night.

Sometimes, ghosts seem to float. Without a human body, they're able to fly and move through walls. And, even though they don't have bodies, ghosts are sometimes said to move objects.

Books fall from shelves. Glass shatters on the floor. Musical instruments seem to play themselves. Sometimes, items go missing. Do we forget where we put objects, or are spirits moving them?

People say they have seen ghost animals and pets. Some have even claimed to see ghost trains and other phantom vehicles.

Chapter 3

CHILLS AND GOOSE BUMPS

Caleb and Mike head into the cemetery. It's late. With the cloud cover, the night is almost pitch black. Town **legend** says ghosts roam the graves at night. Caleb and Mike said they didn't believe it. They also said they weren't scared. So naturally, their friends told them to prove it. All the two have to do is walk across the cemetery. Their friends are waiting on the other side.

As the two walk, they notice the temperature drop. Wearing short sleeves, the boys pick up the pace. But then both get a creepy feeling. Goose bumps cover their skin, but it's not because of the cold. Chills run down their spines. They feel like they're being watched. They're only halfway across, but all it takes is one look at each other to decide: They're sprinting to get out of here!

A common feeling around ghosts is a drop in temperature. Out of nowhere, it gets chilly. You feel cold and get goose bumps. Why does this happen? Ghost experts say this has to do with energies. Spirits need energy to manifest. Heat is a form of energy. The spirits could be pulling heat from the area.

PHANTOM OR FEAR?

Experts blame goose bumps on fear and adrenaline. Adrenaline causes tiny muscles in our skin to tug on hair roots. This makes our hair stand up. And goose bumps form on our skin.

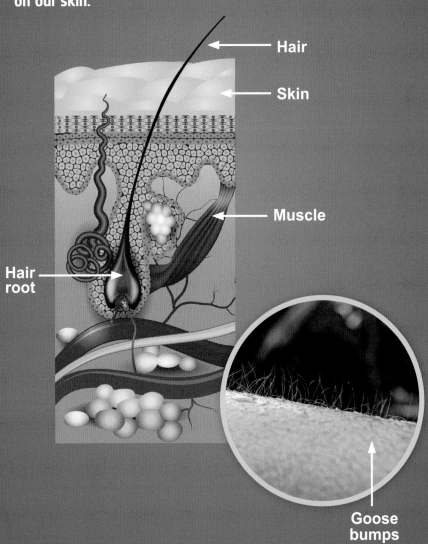

Hair

Skin

Muscle

Hair root

Goose bumps

Chapter 4

SENSING SPIRITS

Cam wakes up in the middle of the night. He could have sworn he heard a voice say "goodnight" to him.

"Mom? Brady?" Cam calls out. But neither his mom nor his brother answers. They're both sleeping in their own rooms, just like every night. Nobody else is in the room with him. Or is someone? Cam feels part of the bed dip down as if someone or something is sitting next to him. Then the weirdest thing happens. It feels like someone is holding his hand. Cam's grandma used to live with them. Before she passed away, she would sit beside Cam, wrap his hand in hers, and say "goodnight" every night before bed.

"Grandma?" Cam asks. He senses her presence for a few seconds more. Then the feeling fades away.

Science claims ghosts aren't real and that there isn't any evidence they exist. So why do we see, hear, and sense ghosts? Scientists say it's because our eyes, ears, and brains play tricks on us. Our brains receive a lot of sights, sounds, and other senses, often all at once. It is normal for us to sense things that aren't actually there. These instances are known as misperceptions. For example, we think we see someone out of the corner of our eye. Or we see shapes or faces in the clouds. Scientists say our brain is simply trying to make sense of what we're seeing.

> The brain finding meaning in meaningless things is known as pareidolia.

FLICKERING LIGHTS

SLAMMING DOORS

TEMPERATURE DROP

DIPPING BEDS

SIGNS OF A GHOST

Many people say they have seen a ghost. But what if you can't see them? These are common signs that a ghost is near.

MUSICAL INSTRUMENTS PLAYING

AN UNSEEN TOUCH

FALLING OBJECTS

SHADOWY FIGURES

VOICES, SCREAMS, OR LAUGHTER

We may all have misperceptions from time to time. We don't pay attention to most of them. But some we blame on ghosts. When we're focused on only one sense, task, or thought, our brains can tune out others. We ignore the things we don't want to see. And we see, hear, smell, or feel the things we do. Some people, like Cam, may think they feel a presence because they want to. They miss the loved one so badly that their mind creates senses.

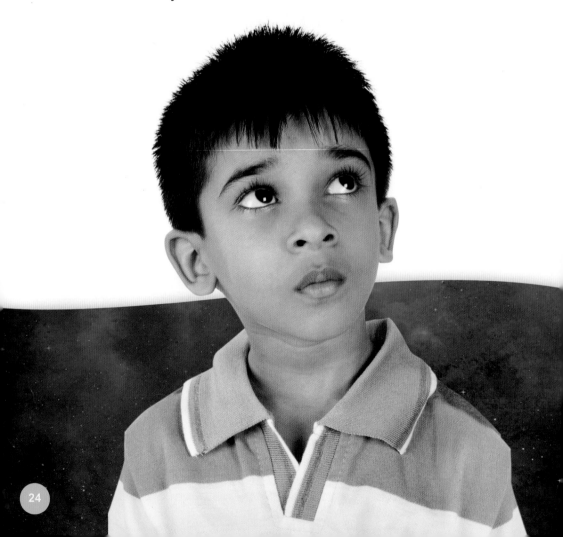

SCARY SLEEP

Experts say sleep paralysis can be the cause of experiences like Cam's. During sleep paralysis, the brain messes up the process of falling asleep or waking up. It can feel like dreaming with your eyes open. Your body feels awake, but it is paralyzed. You can't move, but you can see, hear, or feel figures that may not actually be there.

But is it possible our minds could play such tricks on us? Many who have seen ghosts swear that what they saw was real. Or that what they felt or heard was more than their imaginations.

Could ghosts be real? Maybe some of us are able to sense ghost energies and presences. After all, just because science can't prove something, doesn't mean it doesn't exist. What do you think? Do you believe in ghosts?

GHOST STORIES

Ghost folklore has always been popular. We still tell ghost stories today. People often share and listen to them in dark, spooky settings. Why? It adds to the mystery. Even if people don't believe in ghosts, it can be fun and exciting to imagine them.

BEYOND THE BOOK

After reading the book, it's time to think about what you learned. Try the following exercises to jump-start your ideas.

THINK

FIND OUT MORE. There is so much more to dig up about ghosts. What do you want to learn? Look up sightings on the web, or check out a book from the library. What explanations can you find?

CREATE

ART TIME. Can you draw a ghost? Look up a picture and grab some markers and paper. Will a person see it? What will it be doing? Will it leave behind any clues? The sky is the limit!

SHARE

THE MORE WHO KNOW. Share what you learned about ghosts. Use your own words to write a paragraph. What are the main ideas of this book? What facts from the book can you use to support those ideas? Share your paragraph with a classmate. Do they have any comments or questions?

GROW

DISCOVER! The universe is so large. There are many stories about ghosts. Make a blanket fort or sit around a fire with your family and friends. Share the stories you've heard or make up your own. Who can tell the spookiest story?

RESEARCH NINJA

Visit *www.ninjaresearcher.com/4859* to learn how
to take your research skills and book report writing to the next level!

Research

SEARCH LIKE A PRO
Learn how to use search engines to find useful websites.

FACT OR FAKE
Discover how you can tell a trusted website from an untrustworthy resource.

TEXT DETECTIVE
Explore how to zero in on the information you need most.

SHOW YOUR WORK
Research responsibly—learn how to cite sources.

Write

GET TO THE POINT
Learn how to express your main ideas.

PLAN OF ATTACK
Learn prewriting exercises and create an outline.

FURTHER RESOURCES

BOOKS

Kaminski, Leah. *Can't Rest in Peace*. Minneapolis, Minn.: Bearport Publishing, 2021.

Oachs, Emily Rose. *Ghosts*. Minneapolis, Minn.: Bellwether Media, Inc., 2019.

Polinsky, Paige V. *Ghost Ships*. Minneapolis, Minn.: Bellwether Media, Inc., 2020.

WEBSITES

FACTSURFER

Factsurfer.com gives you a safe, fun way to find more information.

1. Go to www.factsurfer.com.

2. Enter "Ghosts" into the search box and click 🔍

3. Select your book cover to see a list of related websites.

GLOSSARY

adrenaline: a chemical the body produces when you need energy or when you sense danger.

apparition: a ghost or ghostlike image of a person.

distorted: twisted out of a normal shape.

evidence: information and facts that help prove something is true or false.

experts: people who are specially trained or knowledgeable about a certain subject.

flicker: to turn on and off quickly.

folklore: the stories, customs, and beliefs of common people that are handed down from one generation to the next.

interact: to communicate with or involve yourself with another.

legend: a story handed down from earlier times. Legends are often based on fact, but they are not entirely true.

manifest: to make evident by showing or displaying something.

paranormal: supernatural or not scientifically explainable.

phantom vehicles: ghost forms of transportation.

sense: to become aware of something.

translucent: not completely clear. Something that is translucent lets some light through.

INDEX

PHOTO CREDITS

ABOUT THE AUTHOR

Jenna Lee Gleisner is a children's book author and editor who lives in Minnesota. In her spare time, she likes to hike, read, research fun topics like Bigfoot, and spend time with her dog, Norrie.